Name of Look _____

Evening ◯

Daytime ◯

Face

Moisturizer

Concealer

Foundation

Highlight/Blush

Eyes

Brows

Eyelid

Liner

Crease

Mascara

Lips

Liner

Lip Color

Gloss

Notes

Name of Look _____

Evening ◯
Daytime ◯

Face

Moisturizer
_____

Concealer
_____

Foundation
_____

Highlight/Blush
_____

Eyes

Brows
_____

Eyelid
_____

Liner
_____

Crease
_____

Mascara
_____

Lips

Liner
_____

Lip Color
_____

Gloss
_____

Notes

Name of Look _____

Evening ◯

Daytime ◯

Face

Moisturizer

_____

Concealer

_____

Foundation

_____

Highlight/Blush

_____

Eyes

Brows

_____

Eyelid

_____

Liner

_____

Crease

_____

Mascara

_____

Lips

Liner

_____

Lip Color

_____

Gloss

_____

Notes

Name of Look _____

Evening ○

Daytime ○

Face

Moisturizer

Concealer

Foundation

Highlight/Blush

Eyes

Brows

Eyelid

Liner

Crease

Mascara

Lips

Liner

Lip Color

Gloss

Notes

Name of Look

Evening ○

Daytime ○

Face

Moisturizer

Concealer

Foundation

Highlight/Blush

Eyes

Brows

Eyelid

Liner

Crease

Mascara

Lips

Liner

Lip Color

Gloss

Notes

Name of Look _____

Evening ○
Daytime ○

Face

Moisturizer

Concealer

Foundation

Highlight/Blush

Eyes

Brows

Eyelid

Liner

Crease

Mascara

Lips

Liner

Lip Color

Gloss

Notes

Name of Look _____

Evening ◯

Daytime ◯

Face

Moisturizer

Concealer

Foundation

Highlight/Blush

Eyes

Brows

Eyelid

Liner

Crease

Mascara

Lips

Liner

Lip Color

Gloss

Notes

Name of Look ....

Evening ◯
Daytime ◯

Face

Moisturizer

Concealer

Foundation

Highlight/Blush

Eyes

Brows

Eyelid

Liner

Crease

Mascara

Lips

Liner

Lip Color

Gloss

Notes

Name of Look ....

Evening ○
Daytime ○

Face

Moisturizer

....

Concealer

....

Foundation

....

Highlight/Blush

....

Eyes

Brows

....

Eyelid

....

Liner

....

Crease

....

Mascara

....

Lips

Liner

....

Lip Color

....

Gloss

....

Notes

Name of Look _____

Evening ◯

Daytime ◯

Face

Moisturizer

Concealer

Foundation

Highlight/Blush

Eyes

Brows

Eyelid

Liner

Crease

Mascara

Lips

Liner

Lip Color

Gloss

Notes

Name of Look _____

Evening ⭕

Daytime ⭕

Face

Moisturizer
_____

Concealer
_____

Foundation
_____

Highlight/Blush
_____

Eyes

Brows
_____

Eyelid
_____

Liner
_____

Crease
_____

Mascara
_____

Lips

Liner
_____

Lip Color
_____

Gloss
_____

Notes

Name of Look _____

Evening ⚪
Daytime ⚪

Face

Moisturizer

Concealer

Foundation

Highlight/Blush

Eyes

Brows

Eyelid

Liner

Crease

Mascara

Lips

Liner

Lip Color

Gloss

Notes

Name of Look

Evening ○
Daytime ○

Face

Moisturizer

Concealer

Foundation

Highlight/Blush

Eyes

Brows

Eyelid

Liner

Crease

Mascara

Lips

Liner

Lip Color

Gloss

Notes

Name of Look _____

Evening ◯
Daytime ◯

Face
Moisturizer

_____

Concealer

_____

Foundation

_____

Highlight/Blush

_____

Eyes

Brows

_____

Eyelid

_____

Liner

_____

Crease

_____

Mascara

_____

Lips

Liner

_____

Lip Color

_____

Gloss

_____

Notes

Name of Look _____

Evening ◯
Daytime ◯

Face

Moisturizer

Concealer

Foundation

Highlight/Blush

Eyes

Brows

Eyelid

Liner

Crease

Mascara

Lips

Liner

Lip Color

Gloss

Notes

Name of Look _____

Evening ○
Daytime ○

Face

Moisturizer

Concealer

Foundation

Highlight/Blush

Eyes

Brows

Eyelid

Liner

Crease

Mascara

Lips

Liner

Lip Color

Gloss

Notes

Name of Look _____

Evening ⃝

Daytime ⃝

Face

Moisturizer

Concealer

Foundation

Highlight/Blush

Eyes

Brows

Eyelid

Liner

Crease

Mascara

Lips

Liner

Lip Color

Gloss

Notes

Name of Look _____

Evening ◯

Daytime ◯

Face

Moisturizer

_____

Concealer

_____

Foundation

_____

Highlight/Blush

_____

Eyes

Brows

_____

Eyelid

_____

Liner

_____

Crease

_____

Mascara

_____

Lips

Liner

_____

Lip Color

_____

Gloss

_____

Notes

Name of Look _____

Evening ⃝

Daytime ⃝

Face

Moisturizer

_____

Concealer

_____

Foundation

_____

Highlight/Blush

_____

Eyes

Brows

_____

Eyelid

_____

Liner

_____

Crease

_____

Mascara

_____

Lips

Liner

_____

Lip Color

_____

Gloss

_____

Notes

Name of Look _____

Evening ◯
Daytime ◯

Face

Moisturizer

_____

Concealer

_____

Foundation

_____

Highlight/Blush

_____

Eyes

Brows

_____

Eyelid

_____

Liner

_____

Crease

_____

Mascara

_____

Lips

Liner

_____

Lip Color

_____

Gloss

Notes

Name of Look _____

Evening ◯

Daytime ◯

Face

Moisturizer

_____

Concealer

_____

Foundation

_____

Highlight/Blush

_____

Eyes

Brows

_____

Eyelid

_____

Liner

_____

Crease

_____

Mascara

_____

Lips

Liner

_____

Lip Color

_____

Gloss

_____

Notes

Name of Look _____

Evening ◯

Daytime ◯

Face

Moisturizer

_____

Concealer

_____

Foundation

_____

Highlight/Blush

_____

Eyes

Brows

_____

Eyelid

_____

Liner

_____

Crease

_____

Mascara

_____

Lips

Liner

_____

Lip Color

_____

Gloss

_____

Notes

Name of Look _____

Evening ◯

Daytime ◯

Face

Moisturizer

_____

Concealer

_____

Foundation

_____

Highlight/Blush

_____

Eyes

Brows

_____

Eyelid

_____

Liner

_____

Crease

_____

Mascara

_____

Lips

Liner

_____

Lip Color

_____

Gloss

_____

Notes

Name of Look _____

Evening ◯
Daytime ◯

Face

Moisturizer

Concealer

Foundation

Highlight/Blush

Eyes

Brows

Eyelid

Liner

Crease

Mascara

Lips

Liner

Lip Color

Gloss

Notes

Name of Look _____

Evening ◯
Daytime ◯

Face

Moisturizer

_____

Concealer

_____

Foundation

_____

Highlight/Blush

_____

Eyes

Brows

_____

Eyelid

_____

Liner

_____

Crease

_____

Mascara

_____

Lips

Liner

_____

Lip Color

_____

Gloss

_____

Notes

Name of Look _____

Evening ◯

Daytime ◯

Face

Moisturizer

_____

Concealer

_____

Foundation

_____

Highlight/Blush

_____

Eyes

Brows

_____

Eyelid

_____

Liner

_____

Crease

_____

Mascara

_____

Lips

Liner

_____

Lip Color

_____

Gloss

_____

Notes

Name of Look _____

Evening ◯

Daytime ◯

Face

Moisturizer

_____

Concealer

_____

Foundation

_____

Highlight/Blush

_____

Eyes

Brows

_____

Eyelid

_____

Liner

_____

Crease

_____

Mascara

_____

Lips

Liner

_____

Lip Color

_____

Gloss

_____

Notes

Name of Look _____

Evening ◯

Daytime ◯

Face

Moisturizer

_____

Concealer

_____

Foundation

_____

Highlight/Blush

_____

Eyes

Brows

_____

Eyelid

_____

Liner

_____

Crease

_____

Mascara

_____

Lips

Liner

_____

Lip Color

_____

Gloss

_____

Notes

Name of Look _____

Evening ◯

Daytime ◯

Face

Moisturizer

....

Concealer

....

Foundation

....

Highlight/Blush

....

Eyes

Brows

....

Eyelid

....

Liner

....

Crease

....

Mascara

....

Lips

Liner

....

Lip Color

....

Gloss

....

Notes

Name of Look _____

Evening ◯

Daytime ◯

Face

Moisturizer

_____

Concealer

_____

Foundation

_____

Highlight/Blush

_____

Eyes

Brows

_____

Eyelid

_____

Liner

_____

Crease

_____

Mascara

_____

Lips

Liner

_____

Lip Color

_____

Gloss

_____

Notes

Name of Look _____

Evening ◯

Daytime ◯

Face

Moisturizer

Concealer

Foundation

Highlight/Blush

Eyes

Brows

Eyelid

Liner

Crease

Mascara

Lips

Liner

Lip Color

Gloss

Notes

Name of Look _____

Evening ◯

Daytime ◯

Face

Moisturizer

_____

Concealer

_____

Foundation

_____

Highlight/Blush

_____

Eyes

Brows

_____

Eyelid

_____

Liner

_____

Crease

_____

Mascara

_____

Lips

Liner

_____

Lip Color

_____

Gloss

Notes

Name of Look _____

Evening ○

Daytime ○

Face

Moisturizer

Concealer

Foundation

Highlight/Blush

Eyes

Brows

Eyelid

Liner

Crease

Mascara

Lips

Liner

Lip Color

Gloss

Notes

Name of Look _____

Evening ⚪

Daytime ⚪

Face

Moisturizer

_____

Concealer

_____

Foundation

_____

Highlight/Blush

_____

Eyes

Brows

_____

Eyelid

_____

Liner

_____

Crease

_____

Mascara

_____

Lips

Liner

_____

Lip Color

_____

Gloss

_____

Notes

Name of Look _____

Evening ○
Daytime ○

Face

Moisturizer

_____

Concealer

_____

Foundation

_____

Highlight/Blush

_____

Eyes

Brows

_____

Eyelid

_____

Liner

_____

Crease

_____

Mascara

_____

Lips

Liner

_____

Lip Color

_____

Gloss

_____

Notes

Name of Look _____

Evening ◯
Daytime ◯

Face

Moisturizer

Concealer

Foundation

Highlight/Blush

Eyes

Brows

Eyelid

Liner

Crease

Mascara

Lips

Liner

Lip Color

Gloss

Notes

Name of Look _____

Evening ◯

Daytime ◯

Face

Moisturizer

_____

Concealer

_____

Foundation

_____

Highlight/Blush

_____

Eyes

Brows

_____

Eyelid

_____

Liner

_____

Crease

_____

Mascara

_____

Lips

Liner

_____

Lip Color

_____

Gloss

_____

Notes

Name of Look _____

Evening ◯
Daytime ◯

Face

Moisturizer

_____

Concealer

_____

Foundation

_____

Highlight/Blush

_____

Eyes

Brows

_____

Eyelid

_____

Liner

_____

Crease

_____

Mascara

_____

Lips

Liner

_____

Lip Color

_____

Gloss

Notes

Name of Look ....

Evening ⃝

Daytime ⃝

Face

Moisturizer

....

Concealer

....

Foundation

....

Highlight/Blush

....

Eyes

Brows

....

Eyelid

....

Liner

....

Crease

....

Mascara

....

Lips

Liner

....

Lip Color

....

Gloss

....

Notes

Name of Look _____

Evening ◯

Daytime ◯

Face

Moisturizer

_____

Concealer

_____

Foundation

_____

Highlight/Blush

_____

Eyes

Brows

_____

Eyelid

_____

Liner

_____

Crease

_____

Mascara

_____

Lips

Liner

_____

Lip Color

_____

Gloss

_____

Notes

Name of Look _____

Evening ◯

Daytime ◯

Face

Moisturizer

_____

Concealer

_____

Foundation

_____

Highlight/Blush

_____

Eyes

Brows

_____

Eyelid

_____

Liner

_____

Crease

_____

Mascara

_____

Lips

Liner

_____

Lip Color

_____

Gloss

_____

Notes

Name of Look _____

Evening ○

Daytime ○

Face

Moisturizer
_____

Concealer
_____

Foundation
_____

Highlight/Blush
_____

Eyes

Brows
_____

Eyelid
_____

Liner
_____

Crease
_____

Mascara
_____

Lips

Liner
_____

Lip Color
_____

Gloss
_____

Notes

Name of Look _____

Evening ○
Daytime ○

Face

Moisturizer

Concealer

Foundation

Highlight/Blush

Eyes

Brows

Eyelid

Liner

Crease

Mascara

Lips

Liner

Lip Color

Gloss

Notes

Name of Look _____

Evening ◯

Daytime ◯

Face

Moisturizer

_____

Concealer

_____

Foundation

_____

Highlight/Blush

_____

Eyes

Brows

_____

Eyelid

_____

Liner

_____

Crease

_____

Mascara

_____

Lips

Liner

_____

Lip Color

_____

Gloss

_____

Notes

Name of Look _____

Evening ◯
Daytime ◯

Face

Moisturizer
_____

Concealer
_____

Foundation
_____

Highlight/Blush
_____

Eyes

Brows
_____

Eyelid
_____

Liner
_____

Crease
_____

Mascara
_____

Lips

Liner
_____

Lip Color
_____

Gloss
_____

Notes

Name of Look _____

Evening ○

Daytime ○

Face

Moisturizer

_____

Concealer

_____

Foundation

_____

Highlight/Blush

_____

Eyes

Brows

_____

Eyelid

_____

Liner

_____

Crease

_____

Mascara

_____

Lips

Liner

_____

Lip Color

_____

Gloss

_____

Notes

Name of Look ....

Evening ⚪

Daytime ⚪

Face

Moisturizer

Concealer

Foundation

Highlight/Blush

Eyes

Brows

Eyelid

Liner

Crease

Mascara

Lips

Liner

Lip Color

Gloss

Notes

Name of Look _____

Evening ◯

Daytime ◯

Face

Moisturizer

_____

Concealer

_____

Foundation

_____

Highlight/Blush

_____

Eyes

Brows

_____

Eyelid

_____

Liner

_____

Crease

_____

Mascara

_____

Lips

Liner

_____

Lip Color

_____

Gloss

_____

Notes

Name of Look _____

Evening ○

Daytime ○

Face

Moisturizer

Concealer

Foundation

Highlight/Blush

Eyes

Brows

Eyelid

Liner

Crease

Mascara

Lips

Liner

Lip Color

Gloss

Notes

Name of Look _____

Evening ◯

Daytime ◯

Face

Moisturizer

Concealer

Foundation

Highlight/Blush

Eyes

Brows

Eyelid

Liner

Crease

Mascara

Lips

Liner

Lip Color

Gloss

Notes

Name of Look _____

Evening ◯
Daytime ◯

Face

Moisturizer
_____

Concealer
_____

Foundation
_____

Highlight/Blush
_____

Eyes

Brows
_____

Eyelid
_____

Liner
_____

Crease
_____

Mascara
_____

Lips

Liner
_____

Lip Color
_____

Gloss
_____

Notes

Name of Look _____

Evening ◯

Daytime ◯

Face

Moisturizer

_____

Concealer

_____

Foundation

_____

Highlight/Blush

_____

Eyes

Brows

_____

Eyelid

_____

Liner

_____

Crease

_____

Mascara

_____

Lips

Liner

_____

Lip Color

_____

Gloss

_____

Notes

Name of Look

Evening ○
Daytime ○

Face

Moisturizer

Concealer

Foundation

Highlight/Blush

Eyes

Brows

Eyelid

Liner

Crease

Mascara

Lips

Liner

Lip Color

Gloss

Notes

Name of Look _____

Evening ○

Daytime ○

Face

Moisturizer

_____

Concealer

_____

Foundation

_____

Highlight/Blush

_____

Eyes

Brows

_____

Eyelid

_____

Liner

_____

Crease

_____

Mascara

_____

Lips

Liner

_____

Lip Color

_____

Gloss

_____

Notes

Name of Look _____

Evening ○
Daytime ○

Face

Moisturizer
_____

Concealer
_____

Foundation
_____

Highlight/Blush
_____

Eyes

Brows
_____

Eyelid
_____

Liner
_____

Crease
_____

Mascara
_____

Lips

Liner
_____

Lip Color
_____

Gloss
_____

Notes

Name of Look _____

Evening ◯

Daytime ◯

Face

Moisturizer

_____

Concealer

_____

Foundation

_____

Highlight/Blush

_____

Eyes

Brows

_____

Eyelid

_____

Liner

_____

Crease

_____

Mascara

_____

Lips

Liner

_____

Lip Color

_____

Gloss

_____

Notes

Name of Look

Evening ○
Daytime ○

Face

Moisturizer

Concealer

Foundation

Highlight/Blush

Eyes

Brows

Eyelid

Liner

Crease

Mascara

Lips

Liner

Lip Color

Gloss

Notes

Name of Look _____

Evening ⭕

Daytime ⭕

Face

Moisturizer

_____

Concealer

_____

Foundation

_____

Highlight/Blush

_____

Eyes

Brows

_____

Eyelid

_____

Liner

_____

Crease

_____

Mascara

Lips

Liner

_____

Lip Color

_____

Gloss

_____

Notes

Name of Look _____

Evening ○

Daytime ○

Face

Moisturizer

_____

Concealer

_____

Foundation

_____

Highlight/Blush

_____

Eyes

Brows

_____

Eyelid

_____

Liner

_____

Crease

_____

Mascara

_____

Lips

Liner

_____

Lip Color

_____

Gloss

_____

Notes

Name of Look _____

Evening ○

Daytime ○

Face

Moisturizer

_____

Concealer

_____

Foundation

_____

Highlight/Blush

_____

Eyes

Brows

_____

Eyelid

_____

Liner

_____

Crease

_____

Mascara

_____

Lips

Liner

_____

Lip Color

_____

Gloss

_____

Notes

Name of Look _____

Evening ○

Daytime ○

Face

Moisturizer

_____

Concealer

_____

Foundation

_____

Highlight/Blush

_____

Eyes

Brows

_____

Eyelid

_____

Liner

_____

Crease

_____

Mascara

_____

Lips

Liner

_____

Lip Color

_____

Gloss

_____

Notes

Name of Look _____

Evening ○
Daytime ○

Face

Moisturizer

_____

Concealer

_____

Foundation

_____

Highlight/Blush

_____

Eyes

Brows

_____

Eyelid

_____

Liner

_____

Crease

_____

Mascara

_____

Lips

Liner

_____

Lip Color

_____

Gloss

_____

Notes

Name of Look _____

Evening ⚪

Daytime ⚪

Face

Moisturizer

_____

Concealer

_____

Foundation

_____

Highlight/Blush

_____

Eyes

Brows

_____

Eyelid

_____

Liner

_____

Crease

_____

Mascara

_____

Lips

Liner

_____

Lip Color

_____

Gloss

_____

Notes

Name of Look _____

Evening ○

Daytime ○

Face

Moisturizer

_____

Concealer

_____

Foundation

_____

Highlight/Blush

_____

Eyes

Brows

_____

Eyelid

_____

Liner

_____

Crease

_____

Mascara

_____

Lips

Liner

_____

Lip Color

_____

Gloss

_____

Notes

Name of Look _____

Evening ◯

Daytime ◯

Face

Moisturizer
_____

Concealer
_____

Foundation
_____

Highlight/Blush
_____

Eyes

Brows
_____

Eyelid
_____

Liner
_____

Crease
_____

Mascara
_____

Lips

Liner
_____

Lip Color
_____

Gloss
_____

Notes

Name of Look _____

Evening ⚪
Daytime ⚪

Face

Moisturizer

_____

Concealer

_____

Foundation

_____

Highlight/Blush

_____

Eyes

Brows

_____

Eyelid

_____

Liner

_____

Crease

_____

Mascara

_____

Lips

Liner

_____

Lip Color

_____

Gloss

_____

Notes

Name of Look _____

Evening ◯

Daytime ◯

Face

Moisturizer

Concealer

Foundation

Highlight/Blush

Eyes

Brows

Eyelid

Liner

Crease

Mascara

Lips

Liner

Lip Color

Gloss

Notes

Name of Look _____

Evening ◯

Daytime ◯

Face

Moisturizer

_____

Concealer

_____

Foundation

_____

Highlight/Blush

_____

Eyes

Brows

_____

Eyelid

_____

Liner

_____

Crease

_____

Mascara

_____

Lips

Liner

_____

Lip Color

_____

Gloss

_____

Notes

Name of Look ....

Evening ◯

Daytime ◯

Face

Moisturizer

Concealer

Foundation

Highlight/Blush

Eyes

Brows

Eyelid

Liner

Crease

Mascara

Lips

Liner

Lip Color

Gloss

Notes

Name of Look _____

Evening ⭕

Daytime ⭕

Face

Moisturizer

_____

Concealer

_____

Foundation

_____

Highlight/Blush

_____

Eyes

Brows

_____

Eyelid

_____

Liner

_____

Crease

_____

Mascara

_____

Lips

Liner

_____

Lip Color

_____

Gloss

_____

Notes

Name of Look _____

Evening ○

Daytime ○

Face

Moisturizer

_____

Concealer

_____

Foundation

_____

Highlight/Blush

_____

Eyes

Brows

_____

Eyelid

_____

Liner

_____

Crease

_____

Mascara

_____

Lips

Liner

_____

Lip Color

_____

Gloss

_____

Notes

Name of Look _____

Evening ○

Daytime ○

Face

Moisturizer

_____

Concealer

_____

Foundation

_____

Highlight/Blush

_____

Eyes

Brows

_____

Eyelid

_____

Liner

_____

Crease

_____

Mascara

_____

Lips

Liner

_____

Lip Color

_____

Gloss

_____

Notes

Name of Look _____

Evening ◯

Daytime ◯

Face

Moisturizer

_____

Concealer

_____

Foundation

_____

Highlight/Blush

_____

Eyes

Brows

_____

Eyelid

_____

Liner

_____

Crease

_____

Mascara

_____

Lips

Liner

_____

Lip Color

_____

Gloss

_____

Notes

Name of Look _____

Evening ○

Daytime ○

Face

Moisturizer

_____

Concealer

_____

Foundation

_____

Highlight/Blush

_____

Eyes

Brows

_____

Eyelid

_____

Liner

_____

Crease

_____

Mascara

_____

Lips

Liner

_____

Lip Color

_____

Gloss

_____

Notes

Name of Look _____

Evening ◯
Daytime ◯

Face

Moisturizer
_____

Concealer
_____

Foundation
_____

Highlight/Blush
_____

Eyes

Brows
_____

Eyelid
_____

Liner
_____

Crease
_____

Mascara
_____

Lips

Liner
_____

Lip Color
_____

Gloss
_____

Notes

Name of Look _____

Evening ○

Daytime ○

Face

Moisturizer

_____

Concealer

_____

Foundation

_____

Highlight/Blush

_____

Eyes

Brows

_____

Eyelid

_____

Liner

_____

Crease

_____

Mascara

_____

Lips

Liner

_____

Lip Color

_____

Gloss

_____

Notes

Name of Look _____

Evening ⚪

Daytime ⚪

Face

Moisturizer

_____

Concealer

_____

Foundation

_____

Highlight/Blush

_____

Eyes

Brows

_____

Eyelid

_____

Liner

_____

Crease

_____

Mascara

_____

Lips

Liner

_____

Lip Color

_____

Gloss

_____

Notes

Name of Look _____

Evening ⚪

Daytime ⚪

Face

Moisturizer

Concealer

Foundation

Highlight/Blush

Eyes

Brows

Eyelid

Liner

Crease

Mascara

Lips

Liner

Lip Color

Gloss

Notes

Name of Look _____

Evening ○

Daytime ○

Face

Moisturizer

_____

Concealer

_____

Foundation

_____

Highlight/Blush

_____

Eyes

Brows

_____

Eyelid

_____

Liner

_____

Crease

_____

Mascara

_____

Lips

Liner

_____

Lip Color

_____

Gloss

Notes

Name of Look _____

Evening ◯

Daytime ◯

Face

Moisturizer

Concealer

Foundation

Highlight/Blush

Eyes

Brows

Eyelid

Liner

Crease

Mascara

Lips

Liner

Lip Color

Gloss

Notes

Name of Look _____

Evening ○

Daytime ○

Face

Moisturizer

Concealer

Foundation

Highlight/Blush

Eyes

Brows

Eyelid

Liner

Crease

Mascara

Lips

Liner

Lip Color

Gloss

Notes

Name of Look _____

Evening ◯

Daytime ◯

Face

Moisturizer

_____

Concealer

_____

Foundation

_____

Highlight/Blush

_____

Eyes

Brows

_____

Eyelid

_____

Liner

_____

Crease

_____

Mascara

_____

Lips

Liner

_____

Lip Color

_____

Gloss

_____

Notes

Name of Look ....

Evening ◯
Daytime ◯

Face

Moisturizer

Concealer

Foundation

Highlight/Blush

Eyes

Brows

Eyelid

Liner

Crease

Mascara

Lips

Liner

Lip Color

Gloss

Notes

Name of Look _____

Evening ◯

Daytime ◯

Face

Moisturizer

_____

Concealer

_____

Foundation

_____

Highlight/Blush

_____

Eyes

Brows

_____

Eyelid

_____

Liner

_____

Crease

_____

Mascara

_____

Lips

Liner

_____

Lip Color

_____

Gloss

_____

Notes

Name of Look _____

Evening ◯

Daytime ◯

Face

Moisturizer

Concealer

Foundation

Highlight/Blush

Eyes

Brows

Eyelid

Liner

Crease

Mascara

Lips

Liner

Lip Color

Gloss

Notes

Name of Look ....

Evening ◯

Daytime ◯

Face

Moisturizer

Concealer

Foundation

Highlight/Blush

Eyes

Brows

Eyelid

Liner

Crease

Mascara

Lips

Liner

Lip Color

Gloss

Notes

Name of Look _____

Evening ⭘

Daytime ⭘

Face

Moisturizer

Concealer

Foundation

Highlight/Blush

Eyes

Brows

Eyelid

Liner

Crease

Mascara

Lips

Liner

Lip Color

Gloss

Notes

Name of Look _____

Evening ◯

Daytime ◯

Face

Moisturizer

_____

Concealer

_____

Foundation

_____

Highlight/Blush

_____

Eyes

Brows

_____

Eyelid

_____

Liner

_____

Crease

_____

Mascara

_____

Lips

Liner

_____

Lip Color

_____

Gloss

_____

Notes

Name of Look _____

Evening ◯
Daytime ◯

Face

Moisturizer
_____

Concealer
_____

Foundation
_____

Highlight/Blush
_____

Eyes

Brows
_____

Eyelid
_____

Liner
_____

Crease
_____

Mascara
_____

Lips

Liner
_____

Lip Color
_____

Gloss
_____

Notes

Name of Look _____

Evening ⦾

Daytime ⦾

Face

Moisturizer

_____

Concealer

_____

Foundation

_____

Highlight/Blush

_____

Eyes

Brows

_____

Eyelid

_____

Liner

_____

Crease

_____

Mascara

_____

Lips

Liner

_____

Lip Color

_____

Gloss

_____

Notes

Name of Look

Evening ○

Daytime ○

Face

Moisturizer

Concealer

Foundation

Highlight/Blush

Eyes

Brows

Eyelid

Liner

Crease

Mascara

Lips

Liner

Lip Color

Gloss

Notes

Name of Look _____

Evening ◯

Daytime ◯

Face

Moisturizer

_____

Concealer

_____

Foundation

_____

Highlight/Blush

_____

Eyes

Brows

_____

Eyelid

_____

Liner

_____

Crease

_____

Mascara

_____

Lips

Liner

_____

Lip Color

_____

Gloss

_____

Notes

Name of Look _____

Evening ◯

Daytime ◯

Face

Moisturizer

Concealer

Foundation

Highlight/Blush

Eyes

Brows

Eyelid

Liner

Crease

Mascara

Lips

Liner

Lip Color

Gloss

Notes

Name of Look _____

Evening ◯

Daytime ◯

Face

Moisturizer

_____

Concealer

_____

Foundation

_____

Highlight/Blush

_____

Eyes

Brows

_____

Eyelid

_____

Liner

_____

Crease

_____

Mascara

_____

Lips

Liner

_____

Lip Color

_____

Gloss

_____

Notes

Name of Look _____

Evening ◯
Daytime ◯

Face

Moisturizer

Concealer

Foundation

Highlight/Blush

Eyes

Brows

Eyelid

Liner

Crease

Mascara

Lips

Liner

Lip Color

Gloss

Notes

Name of Look _____

Evening ◯

Daytime ◯

Face

Moisturizer

_____

Concealer

_____

Foundation

_____

Highlight/Blush

_____

Eyes

Brows

_____

Eyelid

_____

Liner

_____

Crease

_____

Mascara

_____

Lips

Liner

_____

Lip Color

_____

Gloss

_____

Notes

Name of Look _____

Evening ◯

Daytime ◯

Face

Moisturizer

Concealer

Foundation

Highlight/Blush

Eyes

Brows

Eyelid

Liner

Crease

Mascara

Lips

Liner

Lip Color

Gloss

Notes

Name of Look _____

Evening ◯

Daytime ◯

Face

Moisturizer

_____

Concealer

_____

Foundation

_____

Highlight/Blush

_____

Eyes

Brows

_____

Eyelid

_____

Liner

_____

Crease

_____

Mascara

_____

Lips

Liner

_____

Lip Color

_____

Gloss

_____

Notes

Name of Look _____

Evening ○
Daytime ○

Face

Moisturizer

_____

Concealer

_____

Foundation

_____

Highlight/Blush

_____

Eyes

Brows

_____

Eyelid

_____

Liner

_____

Crease

_____

Mascara

_____

Lips

Liner

_____

Lip Color

_____

Gloss

_____

Notes

Name of Look _____

Evening ○

Daytime ○

Face

Moisturizer

_____

Concealer

_____

Foundation

_____

Highlight/Blush

_____

Eyes

Brows

_____

Eyelid

_____

Liner

_____

Crease

_____

Mascara

_____

Lips

Liner

_____

Lip Color

_____

Gloss

_____

Notes

Made in the USA
Columbia, SC
02 April 2022

58406809R00057